Middle Class to
MILLIONAIRE

Middle Class to
MILLIONAIRE

Making the Leap to the Next Level

David Vernich

COPYRIGHT © 2022 DAVID VERNICH
All rights reserved.

MIDDLE CLASS TO MILLIONAIRE
Making the Leap to the Next Level

ISBN   978-1-5445-3266-0   *Paperback*

         978-1-5445-3267-7   *Ebook*

This book is dedicated to those people who have the guts and the grit to change their family tree by making the leap to become financially self-sufficient and by leaving this world richer by giving way more than they consume.

CONTENTS

FOREWORD — ix

INTRODUCTION — 1

CHAPTER 1
Introducing the Money Scoreboard — 13

CHAPTER 2
The Scale of the Problem — 23

CHAPTER 3
Alternative Investments — 33

CHAPTER 4
The Missing Piece — 41

CHAPTER 5
Don't Copy Mom and Dad — 51

CHAPTER 6
Who, Not How — 61

CHAPTER 7
Face the Fear — 69

CHAPTER 8
The Next Step — 77

APPENDIX
Money Scoreboard Data Sheet — 77

RESOURCES — 91

FOREWORD

DAVID VERNICH
NASHVILLE, MARCH 2022

TWO MASSIVE ISSUES THAT will never be fully resolved in our lifetimes face the majority of the American population:

The retirement income crisis—People are retiring into virtual poverty with insufficient income to maintain the standard of living they had when they worked full time due to a lack of proper financial education.

> The affordable housing crisis—The number of starter homes is declining each year due to obsolescence, gentrification, natural disasters such as fire and floods, and the fact that builders cannot build new starter homes that are both profitable for them and affordable for a buyer. Ultimately, there is no such thing as affordable housing if you simply don't make enough income to pay the average mortgage payment.

Both these problems could be solved—individually and collectively—if every American could learn how to become a millionaire. That might seem crazy, but every individual who has or can attain the status of being solidly in the middle class can absolutely achieve millionaire status.

How do I know that? Because I've seen it. As a bank loan officer, I have watched firsthand as people have made the leap from middle class to millionaire.

And I've done it myself.

At age 45, I was 21 years into my career as a banker, making $80,000 in salary (solidly in the middle class) with a wife and four sons to support. Not exactly rolling in the dough, but not worrying about where my next meal was coming from, either.

After following all the traditional advice (cut your expenses, save more for retirement out of each paycheck, and invest in the stock market through a 401(k) plan offered by your employer) I came to the realization, halfway to retirement age, that it wasn't working. If I kept doing what I was doing, I would probably have to retire in a van down by the river eating a steady diet of government-subsidized cheese, like Chris Farley in his famous Saturday Night Live skit.

Since I implemented the plan I'm about to describe to you in this book, I was able to make the leap from middle class to millionaire. Not only that. I found the process to be fairly painless—and it certainly didn't require superhuman skills to achieve.

Instead of following the sole path we have always had drilled into our heads (which generally only works for very high-income earners), people can add just one missing ingredient to make a huge, life-changing difference in their standard of living.

Spoiler alert: investing in income-producing assets (rental real estate properties) through a partnership of like-minded people who each bring their unique skillsets to the venture will massively increase the probability of becoming a millionaire rather than sticking with a traditional course of action that is guaranteed not to work for the vast majority of people who follow it.

The nice thing about this plan is you can increase your standard of living NOW (you won't have to wait until you are 65 years old to pull money out of your retirement account). You won't have to worry about getting fired from your job (you will have enough income from this strategy to replace your full-time income after a few years) or becoming sick or disabled so you can no longer work, and you will not have to retire (eventually) to a life of tight budgets and a one-way trip to an ever-decreasing standard of living.

As Zig Ziglar once said, "You can have everything in life you want, if you will just help other people get what they want."

I invite you to join me on this quest to learn how to become a millionaire. And once you do, it is our duty to help as many other people as possible to do the same thing, too!

INTRODUCTION

I HATE TO START WITH BAD NEWS, but the vast majority of middle-aged, middle-class Americans have a problem. Maybe not today or tomorrow, or even next year. But sooner or later they're going to have a problem. And by the time they discover what it is, it will be too late to fix it. Their problem is that they have no appreciation of how badly off they'll find themselves after retirement.

As I'm going to show you, there's no need for you to be one of them.

According to the American College of Financial Services, for more than 60 percent of Americans, not formulating and putting a solid strategy into action decades ahead of time for their income needs in retirement *is* their plan. That will add up to a national retirement crisis down the road. And that national crisis will be made up of hundreds of thousands of personal crises as individuals and couples have to cut back on how they live in order to be able to afford to mostly get by on the small percentage of their previous full-time W-2 income that Social Security will pay.

Instead of planning decades ahead for their retirement, most people assume that things will somehow work out. They never do the math. They set out on their career journey assuming that they're going to reach their destination. They're trying to land in Hawaii, but halfway over the ocean they run out of gas. It might be forgivable not to check the gas gauge before takeoff—though it's not really—but they really should have checked mid-flight so they'd know they needed to look out for a place to land far short of their original goal.

Everyone has better things to do than plan their own retirement. Many people don't even open their retirement statements because they know that it's going to be painful to see the small amount of money they have been able to save and how far off-target they really are. They don't want to know the truth. So it's easier to put it off and hope for a fourth-quarter miracle. But you don't want to be throwing Hail Marys for your financial future. It's far better to ask yourself what you can do to make course adjustments now so that even if you don't meet your goal, at least you'll be better off than if you'd ignored the problem until you couldn't do anything about it.

Don't leave it that long. You still have time to fix the problem if you start now, which is why I'm finishing the bad news with an exercise that can help you understand the scale of the problem. It might be more bad news, but once we get this out of the way, we can move on to the good news.

The Social Security Administration has a website where you can check your social security annual statement: www.ssa.gov/myaccount. If you're over 18 years of age, you need to provide your social security number, email, and mailing address, and

INTRODUCTION

it will tell you your projected social security payout at various ages in the future. It will also tell you what estimated retirement income you are likely to receive depending on when you retire. This figure will bring a lot of people up short.

Before you read any more, why not go try it?

■ ■ ■

How did it go? If you are anything like me, you probably just ignored the previous paragraph and carried on reading. Perhaps you said to yourself, *Maybe I'll do that later*. Most people won't, so in the interest of time, let me give you the information I took the time to pull from my own social security statement so we can discuss a real-life example. (But bear in mind that this kind of exercise is *far* more interesting when it's your numbers that are involved, right?)

At this point in my life, I am 59 years old and my social security statement says that my full retirement age is 67. I can claim benefits as early as age 62, but I would take a permanent haircut with the lesser amount of money they would pay me for the rest of my life. I can also delay my benefits until I am 70, which would increase the amount they would pay me.

Here are the figures:

- Age 62 (early payout): $2,116 per month or $25,392 per year
- Age 67 (full retirement age): $3,102 per month or $37,224 per year
- Age 70 (delayed retirement): $3,892 per month or $46,704 per year

If you do this for yourself—and I strongly urge you to do so—don't forget to read the fine print. These are just estimated figures based on a number of factors, but there is one big kicker. I'll quote directly from the social security statement, with my added italics: "By 2035, the payroll taxes collected will be enough to pay *only about 79 percent of scheduled benefits.*"

In other words, all bets are off. Which means you'd better have a better plan to generate income, or receiving even less than the small amount you're entitled to will become your personal reality.

Did you check out your annual statement? If what you saw left you feeling happy about how much income you'll have when you retire, that is awesome. Don't waste your time reading this book. On the other hand, if seeing the reality of your situation has just left you feeling worried, or even sick to the stomach, don't worry. Read on, and let me show you what you can do about it.

HOW WELL-OFF ARE YOU?

The first thing to say is that you're not alone. The vast majority of Americans have no idea how unprepared they are financially for what's coming after they finish work. It's a potentially huge problem that is never discussed. It's quite easy for middle-class people with good jobs and steady income to be wealthy on paper, and even to live in a wealthy way—but it's hugely difficult to save enough money during the course of a working life to be able to enjoy retirement without a drastic reduction of living standards.

INTRODUCTION

That's partly because people tend to overestimate how well-off they are.

Stephen R. Covey explained one of the reasons in his book *The 7 Habits of Highly Effective People*, when he discusses why people often don't accomplish what they want to. He developed a method to categorize your goals into four quadrants, with the squares along the bottom marked very important/not important and those up the side marked urgent/not urgent. Covey says the majority of people spend most of their time in the urgent but not important quadrant, whereas for long-term success they should concentrate on the important but not urgent quadrant. In other words, we tend to put things off when they're not urgent. Things like retirement planning.

People spend more time worrying about the sports team they follow, and the athletes they're hiring and firing, than they do about finding ways to increase their own income.

Another reason is that no one learns anything about personal finance in school. It's treated a bit like sex education; the system is based on assuming that your parents are going to teach you. Schools are more interested in teaching algebra or geometry that you'll never use the rest of your life than how to balance your checkbook or making sure you can earn enough money to not have to struggle financially the rest of your life.

I started this conversation with bad news, because we all have to understand that we have a problem. That will actually eliminate most people who either can't or won't do what is necessary and take corrective action. But that realization is not enough. The next step is figuring out how to change things and then implementing the plan. It's no good knowing we need to diet and exercise to maintain a healthy weight and have a longer life if we don't take steps to put that knowledge into action.

The reality is that most people don't see a lot of benefits immediately, so many give up. They just go home to watch their favorite TV programs. In retirement planning, the equivalent is to think, *Well, I don't have enough money so what's the point? I know I don't have enough money.*

That's not a useful response. The useful response is *What can I do to increase the amount of money I'm making? What can I do to make sure there are no leaks in my financial boat?*

When people go to work for somebody, their employer usually gives them a benefits package, which includes their vacation, sick day allowance, health insurance, and retirement package. That's as far as most people get. That might have worked for your parents, but it's not going to work for you today. The world has changed and there are so many alternative ways to reach your financial goals. That's why good financial planners have become so important, because if you just follow along with what your employer and the government provide you, you'll end up with a Frankenstein's Monster of a financial plan that simply won't achieve the ultimate goal, even if that goal is only a feeling that *I don't want to be poor.*

Like many people, I was in my mid-40s when I began to think about what my retirement would look like in 20 years. I've had a retirement plan since I started work in my early 20s, but as soon as I looked at it in my mid-40s, I saw it would not support my current lifestyle once I retired. When I looked into retirement plans more widely, I saw that most saving, investment, and pension plans are simply not capable of generating the kind of income most people will need in retirement.

Because of my work as a banker, I found a marvelous solution to the problem that's open to anyone with a reliable income or assets and a credit history that will allow them to borrow money from the bank: investing in income-producing real estate.

I've discovered an alternate path that shows people how to leverage their current income, credit score, and various personal assets to invest in real estate acquisition and income-generating real estate so that they can simultaneously both increase their capital assets and generate an ongoing passive income they can enjoy now, many years before retiring full time. And before you start complaining that you're not good at DIY or that you can't hammer a nail straight into a wall, relax. This is a strictly passive investment. You invest, sign a few basic documents, and then wait for the rental checks to arrive. Someone else finds and renovates the properties, identifies tenants, and manages the rentals. You can leave all that to people who are good at it and enjoy it.

MY REAL ESTATE EPIPHANY

I've worked as a loan officer with a number of different banks in the Nashville area for many years, and I've disappointed many people by having to explain that they're not quite as well-off as they seemed on paper. But I've also come across people who have started from scratch and become successful in real estate investing. They bought houses that were maybe 20 or 30 years old, brought them up to current market conditions, then rented them out to young families or people who wanted to live in the area but didn't have the means to buy their own home.

I'd become a banker almost by accident, when my wife went to work at a bank and suggested I'd fit in. I hadn't gotten a business degree, and my math skills weren't that great, but I'd realized early on that banking would bring me into contact with all sorts of other businesses, some of which might give me some kind of economic opportunity. I realized that I didn't want to deal with the headaches that every business owner faces, so I stayed with the bank. But when I'd scared the crap out of myself by looking at my retirement fund, it seemed like a good time to jump in and further investigate the real estate market.

The country's in the middle of a housing crisis. There's a shortage of available real estate, which means there's a growing demand for rental property and a constant supply of tenants. It's also possible to buy properties that are a couple of decades old and renovate them relatively cheaply. If you choose the right properties, you can keep any risk of a devastating loss from the investment very low.

I liked the idea of an investment that helps other people. Providing numerous houses for multiple renters makes me feel better about my retirement savings than, say, investing it all in a tobacco company or a manufacturer of junk food. Housing supplies a basic need and helps overcome a shortage. As a landlord, you supply a service for which people are prepared to pay because they either can't buy property themselves or choose not to.

INTRODUCTION

So I took the plunge. I got a loan—from another bank, not my own bank—and bought a house to renovate.

I hated every minute of it. It was way out of my comfort zone. It required skills I didn't possess. I have a poor track record of almost anything to do with housing. When I selected our first apartment without my wife seeing it first, I had only been shown a model unit and did not bother to look at the actual apartment I had signed a lease to live in until the day we moved in. Surprise! The orange countertops made my wife burst into tears when we walked through the front door of our first apartment as newlyweds. *(Note to self: never again choose a place to live without your wife seeing the property first.)*

It was clear that I would never renovate another house by myself. But it was also clear that the real estate market had a huge amount of potential. I rented the home easily—and my first tenant still lives there today, some 14 years later.

I had to figure out a different way to become involved in real estate investing by using my own unique ability to add value to the process. I had met a couple with exactly the right skills for the task—he was a former architect instructor and pilot, who oversaw the renovation, and she was an accountant, who managed the rentals—who were very successful. I saw a way I could add value to their business. I could bring them passive investors to finance acquisitions so that they could go ahead and locate, renovate, and manage a growing number of properties.

We became partners. Within 14 years, my capital assets in real estate were four times more valuable than the retirement fund that I've paid into for more than twice as long (and still continue to pay into today).

The key is putting together the people with money to invest with the people who do the actual work. A financial planner or a loan officer in a bank can help potential investors with good credit leverage their money by taking loans to finance the process, then using the equity from property appreciation to pay down the loans or to raise more loans for new properties.

Most people are happy to apply for a mortgage for their own personal residence. Then they stop. But that home is not an asset they can use in their retirement, of course, because they have to live in it. Why not change the mindset to think, *I have one mortgage on my own home. Why don't I get another to rent out, so my money can do more work for me?* It's an approach that might make people uncomfortable, as we're brought up to be wary of being in debt, but I'll show you how the risks usually associated with debt can be kept to an absolute minimum.

Real estate investment isn't for everybody. For one thing, it's only an option for someone who can raise money by having a decent income and a good credit history. But that income isn't necessarily as high as you might think, and banks are generally quite happy to lend money for real estate because the property acts as its own collateral, and the rent paid by the tenant will more than cover the loan payment.

There are also parts of the country where it might be more difficult to find tenants. I was recently offered a site in Florida that was so far away from civilization it had no cell phone coverage and the nearest grocery store was miles away. No one is going to be in a hurry to rent somewhere so remote. But even in a depressed area where jobs are scarce and there're not many new people moving in, there's little risk involved as long as you can buy property inexpensively and rent it out cheaply enough to attract tenants.

I'm not going to give you a step-by-step guide about how you find and renovate property. I'm the last person in the world qualified to write *that* book. Nor am I going to tell you to give up your job and sink all your savings into real estate. I still work at the bank, even though my rental income is now greater than my salary, and like any financial planner, I'm a great believer in diversification. You need to be diversified: retirement plans, stock market investments, insurance policies.

I am going to explain in great detail why real estate should be among your primary income-producing assets, and how you can make that happen with the help of some advice from me, but also from other professionals. Financial planners, bankers, and real estate agents are your partners in this venture. They are the people in a position to help you get access to money on the one hand and the market on the other. They're the gatekeepers. I'm going to explain how you can go about real estate investing in a way that will convince them to open the bank vault and let you into a world where your money is working hard to make sure that you won't face a decline in your standard of living when you retire. Or, if you choose to do so, even retire way before old age sets in!

No one wants to retire after a lifetime of work only to find that they're not in a financial position to enjoy the retirement they've waited for so long. This book will tell you how you can avoid that trap. But let's start by looking at why so many of our fellow countrymen and women are so unprepared for what's coming after they give up working.

CHAPTER 1
INTRODUCING THE MONEY SCOREBOARD

WORKING IN A BANK gives me a chance to look into the finances of hundreds of people when they apply for a loan. Over the years, I've learned one thing: most Americans are probably not quite as wealthy as they think. They come into my office believing that they're millionaires, but a lot of them leave feeling disappointed that things aren't quite as rosy as they seemed.

That's OK. You can fix it. But first, you need to understand the problem. And for that, you need to understand a simple concept I call the Money Scoreboard.

Think of your working life as being like a football game. (Stick with me, even if you don't like sports or know much about them—it's a pretty simple metaphor, I promise.)

In this game, you've got 40 working years to increase your retirement account to an amount where it can generate enough passive income (money you make without any active effort, say from owning rental properties or dividends from stocks) to replace the income you're currently living on. That's how much you need to retire with no reduction in your standard of living.

One side of the Money Scoreboard displays your current passive income. It's currently set at 0, because it's still the first quarter and most people's only income early in their career is earned income—what they're paid to do their job. By the end of the game—when you retire from your work—that score needs to match or exceed the passive income you've figured out you need in retirement. (A useful rule of thumb is to start at about your current annual salary.)

The other side of the Money Scoreboard displays your expenses—what it costs for you to live. Typically, that number will be close to your annual salary. If your first job out of college pays $50,000 per year, and you're saving 10 percent, that means you're living on $45,000 per year. In this example, your score is 45 (expenses) to 0 (passive income). You are way behind, big time!

That might look scary, but if you're just starting out, at least you've got the whole rest of the game to catch up. Things get more scary later in the game. What if it's half-time and you're living off $80,000 per year, and your passive income is still at 0? With only two quarters left, 80–0 is a hell of a deficit to make up, so you'd better get mad—and serious. You've got some work to do.

It's not as bad as it looks. Your payout from social security counts as passive income, so you're not at 0. That figure starts rising once you start making contributions from your paycheck, so you can use the social security annual statement we saw in the Introduction (www.ssa.gov/myaccount) to estimate your income from social security when you retire. If you will receive $30,000 when you reach retirement age, your Money Scoreboard is actually 80-30, which looks a lot more promising than 80-0.

Those figures are estimates, however. You don't know how much you're going to be earning 40 years from now or what inflation will be. There's no cause for complacency. It's better to start playing like you're 80 points behind instead of 50 points behind, because it's always better to have more points than you need on the Money Scoreboard.

Nobody wants to look up and realize, *Hey, I've got one quarter (10 years until retirement age) left and I'm behind 80 points.* When that happens, people do desperate, risky things to try to catch up. That doesn't usually end well.

You can't start playing the Money Scoreboard game too early, but you can start it too late. If you want to really understand the game, try filling out your own Money Scoreboard using the data sheet in the appendix at the back of the book.

The other thing that's key to the game is to understand that you're not playing *against* anyone else. This is not "us" versus "them." There's a tendency for people to try to keep up with everyone else. Everyone wants to spend beyond their means to increase their living standards. They see how other people live and they borrow money to do the same, so they can buy nicer cars and bigger houses. Stop comparing yourself to others. If you're always doing that, you're never going to focus on your own situation.

Remember, you only have this one game to play. You have only one financial future to plan: your own. You have 40 years to increase your retirement account so it can generate enough income to replace the income on which you're currently living, or to fund the lifestyle you've decided you want to live as soon as possible and in retirement...and very few people would choose to have a lower standard of living than they have now.

COUNT YOUR ASSETS

I've already said that many middle-aged, middle-class Americans believe that they are millionaires on paper when they're not. They could be. But how do they make the mistake in the first place?

Whenever I assess someone for a potential loan, I treat their tax returns and personal financial statement as a report card of what they've accumulated at this point in their life. That report card can be broken up into three big buckets: how much they have accumulated in real assets, such as cash; how much is in liabilities, or debt; and how much they have saved for retirement.

Most people have an unclear sense of their assets. In *Rich Dad Poor Dad*, Robert Kiyosaki and Sharon L. Lechter gave a simple definition: An asset is something that puts money in your pocket. A liability is something that takes money out of your pocket. Don't make it emotional.

I've seen hundreds of financial statements, and I'm always surprised at the things that people list as an asset. Most often, people list the home they live in as an asset. This is not a true asset if you read the definition of an asset. A property has value, of course, but as long as people are planning to live in that home its value cannot be realized to spend on living expenses. It can't be turned into cash or used for anything else. Its value is likely going up and the loan principal is going down, but that process doesn't put actual spendable money in your pocket until you sell it and have the cash—but then you have to find another place to live.

When someone sells their home, the equity they had in the house becomes an asset they can use to cover living expenses. But they're probably going to take that cash and buy another house—which is not an asset. A home could turn into an asset if you downsize or relocate. For example, you could sell a home in California for $3 million and move to Tennessee, where the same type of home might cost $1 million. Now you've got $2 million in cash. Now that *is* an asset.

One asset people often list that always makes me smile is the death benefit of their term life insurance policy. Again, I don't count it as an asset. By its very definition, they have to be dead to cash it in. In which case, money would be useless to them personally.

When I do my own financial statements, bankers sometimes ask, "But you're not putting anything under personal property?" My response is, "If I sell it in a garage sale and convert it to cash, it will show up in my financial statements. Otherwise, it's not really a financial asset."

Art and jewelry are lovely things to collect and enjoy and potentially pass down to family, but unless you intend to sell them and turn them into cash, they have no real asset value.

The only assets you have are those that put money into your pocket. Period.

If people don't understand that basic fact, it's no wonder they overestimate their own wealth.

HOW MUCH DO I NEED?

Some people do have a million dollars in their retirement account. So they're real millionaires, right?

Not so fast.

Even if you've got a million dollars in your retirement fund, it's not as much as it sounds like (and I do know that it sounds like a lot).

Most people put pre-tax contributions in their retirement account. The idea is that, when they retire, they're not earning a salary anymore so they will be in a lower tax bracket. But that is only true if your income has fallen, and that only works in turn if you can live on far less than what you were making before.

When I retire, I want to maintain the same standard of living I had when I was working, regardless of anything else. In fact, some of my expenses might actually increase. I'll have more time to travel, so I'll spend more on airline tickets, fuel, or nice accommodations. Healthcare expenses also typically rise the older we get, so I'm likely to pay for more prescriptions, more medications and tests, and more doctor appointments. Some will be covered by health insurance, but others won't. In addition, even if your house is paid for and you don't make mortgage payments anymore, you will still have to pay for repairs, insurance, and property taxes.

If you think you're going to be able to live on 80 percent or 70 percent of your pre-tax income, you're likely wrong. Inflation and stock market fluctuations could make you regret that decision down the road.

The reality is that a million-dollar retirement account dwindles very quickly. First, about 30 percent goes to taxes, so it isn't available for living expenses. Now you're down to $700,000. Financial studies recommend expecting about $200,000 in unreimbursed medical expenses and insurance premiums in retirement for someone reaching age 65. That puts another dent in your funds, and you are down to $500,000. If that sum needs to last you 20 years, a conservative estimate for retirement, that means you have $25,000 you can spend each year to live on. That assumes you're not living off the principal, which will of course decrease if you end up spending more than the account earns each year. A more long-term option is to live off the interest your $500,000 generates. If you had a return of 4 percent, you'd have just $20,000 a year, which would put you below the national poverty line.

You would have worked your whole life to retire into a life of virtual poverty.

That million-dollar retirement fund looks a lot less impressive now, doesn't it? I don't say this to suggest there is no hope but to shift your mindset. There's a solution to the problem, once you realize what the problem is.

FINANCIAL SECURITY

Let me try another metaphor. Imagine you're a frog hanging out on a lily pad in a swiftly moving river. Eventually, you realize your lily pad is moving toward a waterfall. Your instinct might be to jump to another lily pad in the opposite direction from the falls, and then to another—but all the lily pads are drifting in the same direction, so you're not addressing the problem. You're just buying a little bit of time.

To solve the problem, you need to jump off the lily pads altogether and leap to the solid ground of the riverbank.

That riverbank is the financial security we all want. And without the right financial plan, it will remain out of reach. The only option will be another lily pad.

Financial security looks different for each individual. It's not a competition between you and anybody else. It's about the life you're living now and the way you intend to live when you stop working for a paycheck. To preserve your lifestyle, your passive income in retirement needs to generate the same amount as your earned income when you were working. If you make $80,000 a year, and you're living on $80,000 a year, then your goal should be to have $80,000 of retirement income a year. If you're making $450,000 per year and spending it, you'll clearly need more income to support that lifestyle in retirement.

Nobody knows how long they're going to live, and people often underestimate how many years they'll spend in retirement. The official full retirement age is now 67. The lower end of the average life span is 87 for women and 85 for men (the wealthier you are, the longer you are likely to live). In terms of mapping out a financial future, I usually suggest that men should plan to live to 90 and women should plan to live to 100.

I've seen this play out with my own parents. Years ago, I asked my father about his life insurance plans. He had a term policy at 65, which meant he was renting it until it expired at age 75. He told me, "I'm not going to need anything past age 70 because I won't be alive."

He just turned 90 last year. In terms of missing it, he wasn't even in the ballpark.

None of us knows what's around the corner, so it makes sense to plan for the longest time possible. Better safe than sorry. Once you've retired, it's difficult to go back and suddenly earn a bit more money to cover yourself.

It's a simple question to ask yourself: would you rather have more money than you need or less?

In reality, most people are about 20 years behind where they should be in their financial preparation for retirement. It's difficult enough to put together a retirement fund of $1 million, but studies now suggest that people need closer to $2 million to cover their expenses. We're trying to play catch-up to a number that keeps growing.

The game's still in play. The Money Scoreboard keeps ticking, whether you're paying attention to it or not. Your opponent's not sitting back and letting you get away with stuff. At the age of 45, you're at halftime in your life. It might feel like you're never going to be able to catch up—but you can.

There are *real* millionaires out there. They are people who can add up all their cash, all their retirement accounts (minus taxes), and all their real estate equity that generates cash flow (not the home they live in) and reach a total well over $1 million. There's no reason you can't become one, too.

I'm going to show you a way it can be done. There are very few guarantees in life; that is true. But I can guarantee that if you don't do something different, you're not going to win the game.

Let's take a closer look at the problem.

CHAPTER 2
THE SCALE OF THE PROBLEM

WE ALL HAVE A NATURAL TENDENCY to focus more on the present than on the future. To paraphrase one of Yuval Noah Harari's ideas from the book *Sapiens: A Brief History of Humankind*: there's not a monkey alive who would trade one banana today for two bananas tomorrow. Having what we need—and want—right now is always going to feel preferable to sacrificing for later. We need to shift our mindset when it comes to saving for retirement, and this plan involves having both what you need now and what you want to have later.

In my experience as a loan officer, there are two different extremes when it comes to people and their money. The first group are the penny pinchers: those people who refuse to spend now with the plan of saving it all for later. The problem with this approach is that life comes with no guarantees. There isn't always a *later*. I'm a big believer in enjoying life now in case there is no tomorrow—because sometimes there isn't. A good friend of mine passed away from brain cancer at 52. They had accumulated almost $10 million in net worth, weren't married, and didn't have any children of their own to leave their wealth to, so they never really got to enjoy the fruits of their labor. My friend worked so hard their whole life saving for a future retirement they never got to experience.

On the flip side are the "rock stars": the people living lavishly in the now without much thought for the later. They're spending as fast as they're earning and banking on the fact that the future is not guaranteed, so why not assume they won't live that long? As I mentioned in Chapter 1, nobody knows how long their retirement—or their lives—will last. You don't want to indulge in the present to the point that you're sacrificing your future livelihood.

There is an alternative approach to just tightening the belt and saving money for 40 years, hoping you live to see the benefit of that hard work. And you don't have to ignore the future and only enjoy the present. There is a more balanced approach that gives you more bananas now—and even more bananas tomorrow.

The beauty of passive income (which is possible to receive from real estate investments) is that it doesn't have a negative impact on your lifestyle now. It doesn't involve sacrificing for your retirement or working more than your full-time job already requires. Instead, it's an approach that allows you to spend—and invest—your current earned income in the same way you always have, while increasing the money you're bringing in, so you can contribute even more to your retirement fund. Or, better yet, you can have an increased standard of living you can enjoy now, not when you are old and unable to travel due to health issues.

WHERE YOU'RE INVESTING

If your current forms of investment are focused on stocks, cash, and insurance, you're probably looking at having the ability to withdraw about 4 percent on average over a long period of time—in other words, about $40,000 on $1 million. But that 4 percent is a conservative estimate and doesn't paint a complete picture. For example, if inflation is 3 percent and you're paying 25 percent in taxes, then you're barely staying even with that 4 percent. That 4 percent rule of thumb is a minimum. And, at this moment in history with non-existent interest being paid on savings, you can't get a steady, reliable 4 percent return anywhere apart from using alternative investments, by which I mean investments different from traditional stock investments, retirement funds, and bank savings accounts.

The truth is that most people don't even know what return they're getting on their investments. When I ask people how much their investments are earning them, they might pull up a statement and say, "This says I'm making 12 percent." A 12 percent appreciation in value isn't bad, but if that can't easily be turned into cash flow without having to sell them or future appreciation can't be guaranteed (which, of course, stocks cannot do consistently year after year), then it might not be as great as it initially sounds. Things that go up can also go down, and the most important thing is to optimize cash flow to live on. Of course any increase is beneficial, whether it comes from dividends, interest, income, or appreciation. Whether it's the stock market or the real estate market, those increases are welcome, but we have to focus on what's going to give us a consistent return and what's going to provide us the cash flow we need to cover our living expenses.

Stock appreciation is unreliable and outside our control. The stock market can be very volatile. When it's in your favor, it can average anywhere from 6 to 12 percent returns, but when you're talking about the entirety of your investment portfolio, that range is wide—and inconsistent. The average temperature where I live in Nashville, Tennessee, is somewhere around 68 degrees, but that average doesn't mean much when I'm living through a freezing winter and the temperature is below 0. Averages only tell you a range; they don't paint a clear picture of the highest highs or the lowest lows.

Consistency and reliability are difficult to control with stock investments. There are times when you do better and times you do worse. The timing of those gains or losses is more important than just expecting an average double-digit return over a long period of time.

■ ■ ■

Thinking about how your investments can turn into cash flow is essential in retirement planning. Your cash flow is what you're using to pay your day-to-day expenses and what you'll continue to need when you retire. That cash flow needs as much reliability and consistency as you can create. Instead of focusing on the return on investment (ROI), what you really need at this stage of your life is reliability of income. You likely wouldn't take a job where the pay varied wildly from month to month, so why put yourself in that kind of situation in retirement? With stock market investments, you spend your working life trying to amass a pool of funds and then, as soon as you retire, your focus becomes all about minimizing loss and converting your funds into an income stream. This is accomplished through capital gains and sales of the stock, but that's not really cash flow. That whole approach is based on hope that the appreciation is enough to eventually let you sell your holdings to somebody else at a higher price and still be able to live off the proceeds. That's fine when it works, but it was not designed to work consistently over a 20- or 30-year period. It's not sustainable for the rest of your life, especially if you have a shot of living to see 100!

WHO YOU'RE INVESTING WITH

When people start contemplating their retirement and investments, they usually want to check in with a financial planner. More often than not, however, a financial planner's first advice is going to be to cut your living expenses and tighten your belt so you can save more money.

After all, financial planners are in the same boat as their clients. They make money from assets under management, so the more assets they have under management, the closer they are to their own retirement. They're making cash flow or commissions off the assets they manage—generally at a rate of 1 percent. If somebody has a million dollars in their retirement account, their financial planner is probably making about

$10,000 a year from looking after them. But the owner of that account, the client, will usually not see a bill for the financial planner's fees: they accumulate more sneakily through commissions, mutual fund kickbacks, fees, and fine print. That's *their* earned income.

In addition, financial planners are under strict guidelines about what they can and cannot do. They are focused on a specific investment path, and they tend to stay on it and encourage their clients to do the same. They rarely talk about real estate as an investment—because there's no commission or incentive for them to do it.

Don't get me wrong: financial planners are valuable at what they do. They can take the money you've earned and saved, organize and streamline it, and send you periodic statements letting you know how your investments are performing. But that's about all they can do. Financial planners are not in the business of increasing your passive income. Think of them like closet organizers: They take your stuff and they sort it into nice, neat piles and stacks, so you can find everything. They promise to keep an eye on it and keep it organized—but you're still responsible for providing the "stuff" to fill up the closet. Your financial planner isn't going to make the closet any bigger or add anything to the contents. They can take care of what you have—to varying degrees—but their job isn't to expand the closet, to fill it with more and more stuff. It's up to you to create your own wealth.

Financial planners and stock investments should be a part of a well-balanced retirement plan; they just shouldn't be the entirety of that plan. Most financial planners would look at what I'm recommending in this book and recognize this is a great way to build wealth. A financial planner knows a plan like mine could be a useful addition to anyone's investment portfolio.

And the plan I'm talking about is still a form of investment. What I do is show people how they can access hidden capital they might not even know they have.

CASH IN ON YOUR ABILITY TO BORROW

As an example, if you want to maintain a middle-class lifestyle in retirement—we'll keep using the $80,000 per year figure—then current predictions and models suggest you would need to have about $2 million in savings. That's a sobering thought. If you factor in social security, although as I've mentioned before that can be shaky at best, you would still need $1,250,000 to generate an additional $50,000 per year in cash flow to live on. Investing in stocks or savings accounts alone isn't likely to get you to that point. But there is potential you might be overlooking.

You have an untapped resource, a secret weapon: your credit and your ability to borrow. You can use that resource to purchase assets that can then generate that ever-important cash flow. Especially when interest rates are low, it's time to seize the opportunity and invest in something that can give you a return both now and in the future.

Most people look at low interest rates from the perspective of a saver—as if those low rates are a punishment affecting the growth of their savings account. I see low interest rates as an opportunity. When interest rates are low, you should be taking advantage by borrowing money to buy additional assets that generate income. Those low rates mean the banks are paying out less in interest, but they also mean the banks are *charging* less in interest too. Low interest rates give you the ability to access money through loans and mortgages and pay less for the privilege. The lower the interest rate, the less you're paying on a mortgage—and the less is coming out of your cash flow from rental property. Remember, a lower interest rate—and smaller mortgage payment—doesn't affect what you charge a tenant; the rental rate is dictated by the market, which is shaped by the law of supply and demand. If your interest rate is lower, then you're simply making more of a profit from that rental income.

Many people have more ability to borrow money than they realize. Do you have a good credit score? Do you have a job with income and a W-2 as proof of that income? Those are both valuable assets to tap into—and if you're not already using them, perhaps you should. Think about it this way: by borrowing a little bit of money now, you have the potential to bolster your income now and massively increase it in the future. To make that happen, start looking into investing in real estate as soon as you are able.

Rental real estate is everywhere, but if you're someone who owns your own home, you might not have thought about it in a while. We're all likely to have paid rent to someone at some point in our lives. The first place I lived after college was an apartment complex, and I was paying rent. I moved from an apartment complex into a newly built duplex, which I rented for a year. Then I went to another duplex, where I was again renting, for years before I bought my first home. I was paying rent to someone every month. Now, I collect rent every month. Ask yourself: which would you prefer, paying rent or receiving it? Rental properties are a direct path to passive income—and passive income is exactly what you need to maintain your lifestyle now and in retirement.

Of course you could save more for your retirement by changing how you live now—like the penny pincher. Or you can choose to not save at all and enjoy now without regard for later—like the rock star. But wouldn't you rather have both? Wouldn't you rather have your banana now, but also put in action a plan for the bananas you're going to need tomorrow, too?

For most people in the middle class, traditional retirement planning methods are not going to be able to achieve your desired standard of living in retirement without making massive cuts to living expenses, so let's look at some alternative forms of investment.

CHAPTER 3

ALTERNATIVE INVESTMENTS

PEOPLE TAKE A VARIETY of approaches to investments, retirement, and financial management. The easiest is the "fast food" approach, which is also the least satisfying—but it's what most people choose. They invest in their employer-sponsored retirement program because, like the drive-through, it involves the least amount of effort, the least amount of thinking, and the simplest return that meets their minimum expectations. Nobody goes through a drive-through expecting the best meal of their lives. And virtually anyone who invests solely through their employer-sponsored retirement program should not expect to build wealth and retire in lavish style.

The benefit of a traditional 401(k) plan with employer match is that the individual has very little involvement and needs to expend no effort. You sign up for the benefit when you're eligible, usually within 30 to 90 days of starting with a company. The money is automatically withheld from your paycheck, and the investment, ostensibly, grows based on the actions and decisions of the team your employer has chosen to manage those funds. You'll get a return, and it might even be a good return.

But no one is as invested in your financial future as you are. The same lack of direct involvement that seems like such a positive for people who don't want to have to make an effort is actually the downside of a traditional 401(k) plan. Nobody involved in that traditional investing process is working toward a goal of increasing your personal wealth, because they don't even know who you are or what you are trying to achieve.

It's in your employer's best interest if you contribute to the 401(k) plan because they're not held liable for guaranteeing you anything when it comes to income in retirement. It's in the best interests of the team who has been hired to manage that portfolio to have more of your money; the more you invest with them, the more assets they have under management that they can charge fees to manage.

Everyone involved in the financial system is making money from your money—regardless of whether you win or lose. In contrast, it seems like common sense that you should only entrust your money to people who have the same incentive as you. This is why it's important to take as much control as you can over your own investments and financial management and partner with people who are incentivized to increase your wealth.

When you hear "control" you might automatically think "hard work." It's true that investing in real estate does involve a level of effort, but it's far from being demanding. It's not labor intensive and it doesn't require you to develop skillsets outside your current abilities. Instead, you just need to start understanding alternative investments.

CONSIDER THE ALTERNATIVES

Diversification is essential for the vitality of any financial portfolio. Nobody has 100 percent of their finances with one company. People have their checking account at one bank, their savings at a different company that offers better rates, and multiple credit cards from various providers. In the same way, no one should have all their assets in the same place. Most financial advisors, as a matter of principle, encourage diversification within your stocks. But if all your money is still invested in the same place—in the stock market, in other words—it's not actually diversified, no matter how varied your portfolio might be. There's nothing wrong with paper assets, but you don't want to rely solely on them.

The same is true of so-called "alternative investments." Despite their name, they're not some kind of fringe activity. They're investments such as gold and silver commodities, or crypto currencies. They're different from the traditional products and investments offered by most financial advisors—who tend to steer clear of them because they are outside the usual investment portfolio—but ultimately they're not that much different. They might increase in value over time, but you can only realize that value by selling them off, which obviously means they won't be gaining value for you any longer, because you won't have them.

What they are not really designed to do is to generate cash flow for you to live off as you get older. The only form of alternative investment that can do that is investing in real estate. The only area that offers a growth in value *plus* an ongoing, stable passive income is real estate investing.

It's possible to invest in real estate in ways other than by directly purchasing property, of course. For example, you could pursue a real estate investment trust as an option, where you contribute to a trust that owns the property. However, a real estate investment trust is, essentially, no different from investing in the stock market. Real estate is packaged into a trust managed by a trustee. Your investment in the trust will earn you a portion of the cash flow as a dividend, and because the real estate is being bought with leverage from institutional debt, there's a higher return. The real estate your money is invested in doesn't belong to you, however. You don't own any physical assets—you simply own a portion of the equity. Investing for yourself in rental properties, on the other hand, will give you a tangible asset that appreciates in value.

THE "REAL" IN REAL ESTATE

Most people don't really know where or how their money is invested. When you ask someone about their stock investments, they might be able to tell you the financial firm handling their portfolio. They might even be able to tell you some of the stocks in which their money is invested or some of the gains—or losses—their accounts have had. But that's rare, and it's generally limited to the people who quite enjoy devoting time and energy to that sort of deep dive into the market. No matter what, they can't physically *show you* their investment since it is generally a statement with some numbers.

With investments in rental property in your local area, you don't have to track price changes and revenues online. You can physically drive by the property. You know the name of the family who lives there. You might even know the factory where they work and their annual salary, because they provided that information when they applied to rent the property as their home. That property—that home—is tangible and real, something you can touch and see. Everything is very physical and "real." And ultimately, that tangibility means you're getting more for your investment and taking less risk because the property has an underlying real value—which no stock does.

There will be a constant demand for property. This is especially true right now. The real estate market is hot, and values are increasing tremendously. This is all due to one thing: supply and demand. If there's a limited pool of something, there are automatically more buyers chasing that thing who are prepared to pay more to get it. And, right now, there's a vast shortage of affordable housing and starter homes in the United States, which creates a great opportunity for investors.

Interestingly, the reason we're in this position with housing in America has to do with one of the most notorious events in recent financial history: the property crash of 2008. But that financial disaster has actually created a market of opportunity and had more to do with how the debt was structured than the real estate it was used to purchase.

THE US HOUSING BUBBLE

Essentially, the 2008 property crash was a result of a combination of greed and a lack of financial knowledge. There was a big push in the years leading up to the crash to help more Americans become homeowners, but lending institutions did so by relaxing lending standards and packaging mortgages that depended on investors to buy them as investments. The entire system, however, was dependent on one thing: people being able to pay their mortgages. Those people were destined to fail at that because of the way the mortgages were packaged.

Buyers were given a low "teaser" interest rate for their loan, which was only good for a few years. Then the rate would reset to a future higher rate. Instead of lending institutions working with borrowers to secure a 30-year fixed rate mortgage people could afford, Wall Street institutions got greedy and were basically subsidizing loans to get buyers into a home right away. They rationalized this approach by encouraging buyers to believe that they would be able to refinance in the future when the property appreciated in value. When the interest rates reset and people inevitably defaulted on those loans, the whole thing collapsed.

The real estate market is still playing catch-up today. A certain number of houses have to be built to keep the inventory stable, but the financial collapse took out so many developers, lenders, and buyers that the inventory was no longer sustained. Some estimates indicate that the housing industry is about three million properties short of where it should be right now. But that decrease in supply has led to an increase in demand due to demographics.

There's a gap in affordable housing right now that's creating a perfect scenario for real estate investors. The new homes being built today are not the "starter homes" that first-time home buyers can afford. Construction firms put their efforts into higher end properties with bigger profit margins. Although everyone wants to live in a brand-new house, most people can't afford to purchase or build one of these new homes. They've been priced out of the market.

Those same people would often be able to buy an older home, but they are resistant to buy them—especially if the property requires repairs and updates. The market is full of homes in the 20-year and 30-year range. They need renovations—more expense and aggravation—but they all have great potential. Those properties can easily become rentable or sellable, if you have the right team and can secure the financing.

Even at the lowest point of the 2008 financial crisis, when there were foreclosures everywhere, the price of houses dropped, and the value of properties dove even lower, one thing didn't change: rents. There were staggering numbers of foreclosures, and banks were having to decrease house prices because they couldn't sell them. The market was upside down. But if a house was rentable, you could rent it to tenants. The cash flow a property generated was not affected by a drop in the property's overall value. Rents were still the same.

People need affordable housing, and renters will always be in the market. That's something you can trust. For me that's preferable to trusting that if I devote 10 percent of my paycheck to Wall Street throughout my working life I can expect enough money to be there for me to live on one day. I don't trust a process where someone else is in control of my money, where someone else is tasked with helping me meet my financial goals. I want to be the one in charge of my income now and the income I know I'll need in retirement.

THE POTENTIAL OF INVESTING

Various types of alternative investments seem to offer greater returns than traditional investments, but virtually all of them have their own drawbacks. In virtually all types of investment and retirement plans, it's the bankers, brokers, and administrators who are making money, regardless of whether you are.

Rentable real estate is a known physical asset that will generate an income stream. The best part is, it's ultimately a passive approach. It doesn't involve much more effort than the "fast food" approach, but this time you're not at the drive-through, you're at the farmers market picking exactly the gourmet ingredients you want. You manage the cash flow from the tenant and you keep the property maintained. Other than that, as long as your renter is paying their rent, there's not a whole lot you have to do. With a well-maintained property you've updated and a reliable tenant you've vetted, you can sit back. And that kind of passive income can pave the way for your financial future.

CHAPTER 4

THE MISSING PIECE

THE FIRST RENTAL PROPERTY I ever bought has had the same tenant for over 14 years. I've used the rental income to pay the mortgage on that property—interest and principal—so today I continue to receive passive income in monthly rent, which is just flowing directly into my checking account. Of course that kind of situation isn't necessarily typical—I lucked out for a first-timer—but in today's market, good property management can attract long-term tenants.

This is particularly true because there are so many bad property managers out there. It's worth it to a renter to stay somewhere long-term if the property manager is responsive and treats them well. Most renters want the same kind of stability as home owners—they're just achieving it in a different way.

To be a good property manager, all you have to do is fix something when you say you'll fix it and answer emails or phone calls from tenants when they reach out to you. Taking care of your tenant is an important part of being a landlord, because taking care of your renter is indirectly taking care of your property—and therefore your investment.

Of course, having a long-term renter in place likely means that there has not been a huge increase in the monthly rent for a property over the duration of the rental. But when you have a tenant who pays reliably and takes care of the home, it's worth keeping the rent consistent as long as they're willing to stay. Approaching rental property with that mindset reaps positive rewards, because as long as you don't give your tenants a reason to leave, they generally won't leave.

Once you've purchased a property and renovated it to make it rentable, you can usually map out the anticipated expenses for the future. Commercial mortgages are locked in for five years, and the only variables on the expense side that might go up are property taxes—which are controlled by the county—and insurance, although if you don't have any claims, that will stay relatively the same. Otherwise, you only have repairs and maintenance, and if you've renovated the property in advance of renting it, both those costs should be negligible. Because your major expenses are not increasing, you're not under any pressure to increase the rent every time a lease is up for renewal as long as a reliable renter is happy in your property and paying their rent regularly.

THE NEED FOR AFFORDABLE HOUSING

The opportunity to make money from home rentals is a consequence of changes in the real estate market. There's a huge demand from renters seeking housing right now because it seems that no one can afford to build affordable homes today.

Today's new construction is almost exclusively aimed at the executive or luxury market, while the supply of affordable housing relies on renovating stock that was built 20 or 30 years ago.

This demand for affordable housing has created a huge market opportunity—and it's one that you can enter using leverage. Real estate is virtually the only investment of which that's true. You're only putting 20 percent of the money down, and the bank puts in the rest. If you have equity in the home you live in, or in other property, you might not even need to put that 20 percent down in hard cash. A line of credit means you're only leveraging the bank's money, not yours. Because, in the current market environment, the bank charges roughly 4 percent on investment property, it's a self-liquidating asset for the loan.

Real estate will start paying dividends back to you as soon as you invest. A new home builder I know explained his three avenues to profit to me. First, he builds new houses and sells them retail. Second, if a house doesn't sell retail, he can offer a lease-to-purchase option, which essentially lets somebody into the house, where they can lock in the price for three to five years as a renter. His third option is simply renting out the properties he builds. All three methods earn him income on whatever property he's built, so he has never lost money on a house.

In spite of the horror stories we've all heard, there's never any reason to lose money on a house. It's all about not overpaying, holding on, and waiting long enough. As long as you're buying in the right areas, there will always be demand. The same builder told me that at one time between 15 and 20 percent of new construction was considered "starter homes," affordable housing for first-time buyers. Now, that percentage has fallen by half, to 10 percent or under. Land is so expensive that builders are switching to apartments and large developments where they can include more housing on a given piece of land, because more density means more profits for the builders.

But that also means that the vast majority of existing single-family homes built 20 to 30 years ago that come on the market are ripe for rental property investment.

The housing market used to be full of families and individuals buying their first home where they'd stay for 30 years, funded by a 30-year fixed-rate mortgage. That doesn't happen as much anymore. The market is changing. Some people find the down payment required for a mortgage prohibitive; others simply don't want to go through the paperwork nightmare of securing a mortgage; others would find it difficult to get a mortgage for reasons that are no fault of their own. The result is that more people are looking to rent instead of buy.

Despite this shift in the market, the gold standard for many people remains to live in a single-family home with no shared walls and at least a small yard to enjoy. It's the upbringing many people had, and the dream for them and others, and demand for such properties will never disappear—even if the path to living in them is more likely through renting than through a down payment and a mortgage.

INVESTING WITH OPEN EYES

To make the most of your investment, it is essential to know your market, but the math involved in making sure you make a sensible purchasing decision is fairly simple. Learn what the average income is in a given area and the average rent that people pay for various types of property. Determine what kind of return you're looking for, and then do the math. For example, if you want to get 12 percent gross per year and typical rent in the area you're looking to buy is $1,000 per month, then you're looking for a house with an investment of $100,000 (that should be your total expenditure, so the figure should include both purchasing the home and making the necessary renovations).

Compared to other investment opportunities, the timeline with rental properties is usually far quicker, although that will vary depending on the market and the team you have doing the work. In general, assuming a property requires a little work, I build in about four to six months to get the house ready. The property should be empty while you're doing initial repairs and maintenance, but as soon as it's presentable you can start putting it on the market. If the real estate market in an area is good, the rental market in the same area will also be good. My rule of thumb is that, if I start advertising a new property at the beginning of the month, my goal is to have a renter in place by the beginning of the next month.

The key is making sure you know your numbers. Do the math and know what your holding costs on a property are going to be based on the repairs needed and the rental market. "Holding costs" are what it costs from when you take ownership of the property until the time when you start making money on it, which might include payments on a loan or line of credit, utility expenses, contractor payments, and so on. If you set up a credit line based on the equity in your own home, or down the line on your other rental properties, then the money for those holding costs is covered by that loan, rather than coming out of your own personal bank account. As an added bonus, all those expenses—interest, repairs, and whatever—are tax deductible.

HOW REAL ESTATE CHANGED MY FINANCIAL APPROACH

Once I saw the power of real estate firsthand, I set myself a goal of owning 10 houses by the time I retired.

The math was simple. I've been working since I was 22 years old, and all that time I've been contributing to my retirement plan. When I was 45, however, I had the sudden realization that those methods were not going to set me up for the retirement I wanted to enjoy. At that point, I had 23 years of accumulated retirement savings and no real estate apart from my family home. That was when I started investing in rental properties, while still contributing to my retirement account through my employer. Fourteen years later, the total of my real estate equity is 4.5 times more than the value of my retirement account, even after having a 23-year head start on the 401(k)!

A property portfolio doesn't just generate passive income from rent. There's usually an absolute increase in value, too, and these potential increases can be remarkable. I purchased a small single-family home of around 940 square feet for around $60,000 and spent another $25,000 to renovate it. About four years later, I had an appraisal done that valued the house at $180,000, which was great given what I'd paid just a few years earlier. A word of warning, however: an appraisal is just that—a statement of *potential* value, not the true value of the property. The appraiser isn't offering to give you that amount of money—and it's possible no one else will either. The true market value of a property is what someone else will pay to buy it, and you won't know that until you sell it.

We rented that single-family home for nine years straight without any issues. Then, our tenants in the house told us they were giving up their lease because they had qualified for a mortgage and were going to buy a home of their own. Their departure led us to assess the market in the area where the house was, where we knew inventory was very tight. We brought in a real estate agent, not an appraiser, to see what the house might sell for. She said that if we put $3,000–$5,000 into the property for landscaping, painting, and other cosmetic upgrades, she'd be able to sell the house for $240,000. Two weeks later, after the improvements, the market had grown even hotter, and she put the house on the market for $260,000. She had five showings, which resulted in three offers, and we eventually accepted a full cash offer of $280,000—for a house we'd invested $85,000 in and had been collecting rent from for nine years.

The more you invest in rental properties, the more secure your investments become. For example, if I have one property and one tenant, and that tenant doesn't pay rent or starts to create problems with the property, then 100 percent of my rental properties have become an issue I need to deal with. When I have multiple properties and experience problems with an individual tenant—and I'll repeat that that doesn't happen that often with good property management—that one problem concerns only a fraction of my properties while the others are no trouble at all. Any loss I take or additional investment I need to make in that one property will be offset by the steady income from all the other properties. Owning multiple properties and receiving multiple rents also ensures that you have the cash flow to deal with any problems that arise with specific homes.

THE POWER IN REAL ESTATE

Banks love to lend money on real estate. I've already mentioned that it's the only form of investment where you can leverage other people's money, but most people don't realize how much borrowing power they have when purchasing property. As a banker myself, I can tell you: real estate is a bank's all-time favorite collateral! Any financing through a bank needs some form of collateral, and real estate is any banker's preferred form. Banks and brokerages only lend 50 to 65 percent on a stock portfolio, but banks will lend up to 80 percent on real estate.

Real estate provides the greatest lending power because it's a tangible asset that generally appreciates in value. When real estate is attached to financing, banks can be certain that they will get their money back. In those situations, the leverage is actually in the borrower's favor.

Most people who own a home, earn a steady income, and have good credit are in a very strong position to invest in real estate. What puts them off is fear. They've been conditioned to believe that the lending institutions have all the leverage, which simply isn't the case. The traditional line of thinking about money and debt has always been, *If you don't have the cash on hand, don't buy it.* But the world has changed dramatically since that concept first took hold. The system has changed to accommodate debt and make it less unstable, so banking and the market look very different now from they did when our parents were young adults.

We've been conditioned to believe that all debt is bad, and that's just not true. I learned from Robert Kiyosaki and Sharon L. Lechter's *Rich Dad Poor Dad* that there are actually two different kinds of debt: good debt and bad debt. In the most basic terms, good debt is debt that somebody else pays for, like a mortgage on a property that is being paid by a tenant paying rent to you for living there. Bad debt is when you've borrowed and have to pay out of your own paycheck, like a loan for a car. If we insist on seeing all debt as bad debt, we prevent ourselves from ever borrowing any money except for what we absolutely need. That kind of approach is closing us off from opportunities that can actually help us build wealth and secure a more stable financial future.

Real estate is one of the only asset classes that will generate income now through rent and into the future through both rent and appreciation in value. And the first step to unlocking that value is to unlearn some of the attitudes toward money and wealth we learned from previous generations.

CHAPTER 5

DON'T COPY MOM AND DAD

MOST OF US LEARNED our attitudes toward money from our parents and the way we saw them managing their household finances. My parents definitely had a different approach to finances than mine. Even today, my mother experiences more satisfaction from seeing their money sitting in a bank account than she would from actually spending it—which she could afford to. My father, meanwhile, is convinced the entire banking system will collapse at any moment and has been known to keep cash in a filing cabinet drawer rather than trusting it to a bank. Or, again, spending it on himself and my mother.

When I was growing up, my parents were always tight with their money. They had experienced the Great Depression, and in their minds, money was a scarce commodity—and so were all the resources and possessions it could buy. If I didn't know better, I would swear that it was my parents who invented the adage "Money doesn't grow on trees." I absolutely agree that money doesn't grow on trees, but it does exist in a far more plentiful supply than most people realize. The issue about money isn't about supply; the issue is about mindset.

THINK LIKE A BANK

Americans have been brought up with a fear of debt, a belief that owing somebody anything is far worse than getting negligible returns on an investment. When you're afraid of debt and believe that money is scarce in the world, it's inevitable that your options can feel very limited. Most people in that mindset figure that their best approach to a financially secure life is to cut their expenses to the bone and put as much money as possible safely in a bank, where it will maybe earn them some interest. But the interest money will earn in a bank is rarely going to amount to much, especially once you factor in inflation, so this scenario doesn't benefit depositors: it only benefits the banks. If depositors keep money in a savings account with a bank, the bank is essentially borrowing their money—and paying very little interest to do so.

Banks aren't going to pay you well for your money because they don't need to. That's because right now money is abundant in the world, thanks to a fiat system in which no actual commodity backs the currency. Central banks are simply trying to manage their national economies to ensure that any recessions are short-lived, and they do this by controlling interest rates and money supply, which they can increase if they want to. The system means that banks have all the power, rather than their customers.

Instead of thinking like a customer, you've got to start thinking like a bank. Once you realize that depositing money and hoping for a return from it isn't getting you where you want to go because it's out of your control, you can focus on the leverage and power you do have. Use your job, your W-2 income, and your credit to borrow money *from* the bank rather than deposit money *in* the bank. Instead of the bank paying you a tiny pittance on the money you've lent to them by putting it in a savings account, you can pay the bank a modest interest rate for the money you borrow from them to go out and create a source of passive income for yourself.

The beauty of real estate loans is that you're only responsible for your share of any potential future loss, not for 100 percent of the total loan amount. This lessens the income you receive, of course, because the bank takes its share in terms of mortgage interest, but it also reduces the risk by making you responsible for only a small portion of the money borrowed. The bank might get the interest on the loans it makes you, but you get all the rental income the investment produces, plus the reward of 100 percent of any appreciation in the value of the real estate. All the bank gets back is the interest repayment, which is an amount that grows smaller every year as you pay down the principal balance.

This approach makes becoming a millionaire quite simple. If you have the ability to borrow a million dollars and pay it off, then at some point, you will be left with a million-dollar asset—the value of your property holdings without even considering any appreciation.

If it's so simple to make money this way, why isn't everyone doing it? Because of the way our culture and previous generations have approached money and debt.

WHEN THE HARD PATH BECOMES EASY

Another barrier to people becoming involved in owning and managing rental property is that it can seem daunting. It doesn't appear on the surface like a particularly easy way to build wealth. Any time there's a fork in the road with two paths—one of them hard and one of them easy—most of us consistently choose the easy way. But, as I've often told my own children, what we often don't realize—and what has taken me a long time to realize myself—is that, with time, the hard way becomes easy; but the easy way, over time, can become difficult.

I considered investing in rental property for years before I took the plunge. A huge part of my resistance came from the fact that real estate investing was something new. I'd never done it before, and the unfamiliar is always harder than what we know. I now know that, by overlooking a path that would take me where I wanted to be financially for so long, I was taking something relatively easy and making it hard.

There are many reasons you might feel reluctant to get involved in real estate—and almost all of them are due to misinformation. The last thing my father could imagine doing is buying a rental property. And he could tell you every reason in the world why it wouldn't work. However, he'd also choose to simply overlook all the reasons it could work, because his mindset hasn't shifted from the world he grew up in.

One issue with shifting the mindset about real estate investment comes from the idea that in order to be a property owner you need to have special skills: to be a skilled construction worker, a real estate guru, an interior designer, a property manager. People tend to imagine all the tasks they think are involved in buying properties, renovating them, and then renting them—and they cannot imagine themselves doing them all and doing them well.

The great news is that we don't have to. There's a psychological barrier that leads us to believe the only way we can do something is if we can do it all on our own. It's another throwback to a time when everyone was determined to be completely self-reliant. We feel a need to master all the skills and abilities and knowledge required to complete the entirety of a task before we even take the first step toward completing it. But you don't need to do everything yourself. In fact, you really shouldn't be doing everything yourself at all. You need to find a team.

I've worked in banking my entire career. I know about preparing financial documents to secure financing. I know about the forms that need to be filled out, the documentation that needs to be submitted, the approaches and collateral that reach the desired outcome. Those things are second nature to me because I've been dealing with them for years. There are plenty of people in the world, in contrast, who would recoil at the idea of filling out loan paperwork or gathering supporting documents to try to obtain financing. Going to a bank and dealing with a lender would be their idea of a nightmare. It's a walk in the park for me.

We all have our own superpowers, the contributions we can make to a team. It's only by putting together people with a variety of abilities that complement one another that you can make a task far easier and more manageable. Can you imagine any scenario where an individual soccer player is ever going to beat an entire soccer team—even a mediocre one—all by themselves?

In terms of real estate, figure out the skillsets you can bring to finding, buying, and renovating a property. Then determine what other skillsets you need, and go out and find people who have those skills. You don't have to learn how to do everything to make a real estate rental business work; you just have to learn how to find the right people to join your team.

DON'T QUIT YOUR DAY JOB

If you're in a position to borrow money to purchase rental real estate, you almost certainly have a current day job, meaning that it's something you are paid for that takes up your full-time responsibility. On the one hand, that's great because it gives you the security to have borrowing power. On the other hand, you will reach a point in almost any career where you will max out your earnings. There are only so many promotions and so many pay increases anyone will receive beyond the standard cost-of-living adjustments (and don't forget that inflation is always lurking out there, quickly diminishing any kind of salary gain we think we've received). You will inevitably reach a point where you simply can't rely on your day job to substantially increase your income—or your retirement plan. That's why you're exploring the strategy of adding real estate investment to your mix of assets.

That doesn't mean you quit your day job. I held on to my banking job throughout my entire real estate investment career. That was partly because I like to keep busy—and I enjoy my job—but also because my goal was never to "not work" prior to my retirement. My goal was always to increase my income, and it was only when I realized that my day job wasn't going to accomplish that that I started pursuing other options.

I didn't want to stop working. Like most other people, I decided that the best solution to the problem was finding a side gig. In the current gig economy, there are many options for what that can look like, but most traditional side gigs will take up even more hours of your time for a minimal hourly wage. Very few will lead to the kind of passive income and wealth you want to manifest for your future.

The only one that will produce these desired results is owning rental properties.

Investing in real estate might involve a lot of work upfront—researching the market, finding a property, making the necessary renovations, organizing the rental and property management—but once the majority of that work is done, it requires very little time and energy to simply collect the rent. All the work happens on the front end, and then there's nothing to do but collect the rent and receive the capital appreciation later. The investment pays dividends for years to come. You leverage time: other people are working at their job to pay rent to you on your property, and that passive income helps contribute to your retirement income.

Managing rental property is not a get-rich-quick scheme or a passing phase. It's a tried-and-true plan to grow your wealth that has worked for millions of people. Whenever you go to work or drive to the grocery store, you are passing hundreds of houses, apartments, and other properties that are being rented. There's a huge variety of reasons that people choose to rent rather than buy—anything from lack of financing eligibility to needing to be flexible in where they live for their careers—and that means that there are always going to be plenty of renters in the world. They're not in short supply any more than money is.

You don't have to have special skills or a contact list of the right connections to begin to benefit from their availability. All you have to do is find a house that somebody would want to live in and would pay for over time. That's it.

THE NEW FINANCIAL GENERATION

If I had approached my mom and dad when I began my real estate investing career and told them my plan, they'd have laughed at me. If I'd said that a dozen years down the line I'd have millions of dollars of assets and access to millions more dollars in credit, they would have looked at me as if I was crazy. All they would have seen in my plan was the risk, and in their minds all that risk would have been sitting squarely on my shoulders, leaving me in a precarious position with no way out. But that's just not a true picture of reality.

I sometimes tell people that, with my parents, the often-told story of whether someone sees a glass with some water in it as half full or half empty, the answer is neither. For my parents, the glass is completely empty. Not only that, it's got a crack in it, so it will never hold liquid again.

My mother has never been able to fathom the idea of someone having a million dollars. She has said before, "How could someone possibly spend a million dollars in a lifetime?" It is beyond her realm of thinking, because that way of thinking hasn't progressed as the economy has changed. My method of investment brings becoming a millionaire within reach for even those with middle-class incomes.

For me, the key to unlocking the potential wealth in rental properties wasn't just about figuring out the right investments; it was recognizing that I didn't need to do all the work myself. I just needed to assemble a team and find the right people to work with. Let's look at how you can do that, too.

CHAPTER 6

WHO, NOT HOW

WHEN I PURCHASED AND RENOVATED my first rental house, I hated the whole process. I tried to do it on my own, and it was too much work—and work I didn't enjoy. I decided right then that I never wanted to do it again. It was only when I started sharing the work with professionals that my whole attitude changed and this new method became clear and started to work for me.

Ever since that first house, I have worked with partners. No one sought me out to guide me through the process, so I had to reach out and find knowledgeable individuals who would be willing to teach me. My experience with the first rental house had shown me that I had a lot to learn. The first people I reached out to were actually people I knew from my work in the banking industry—people who I knew were already making a full-time living from investing in real estate.

Gurus in real estate sometimes say, "If I can do it, anyone can do it!" That's a bit misleading. Yes, anyone can do it—but that doesn't mean anyone can do it *well*. We all have our own skills and strengths, and we also all have our limitations. But for every skill we lack, there's somebody out there who possesses it. And for every strength we provide, there's somebody out there who doesn't have that same ability and would benefit from us working with them.

The key is to know your own strengths and weaknesses. We have to ask ourselves, *What skills do I have to offer that can add value to this process? What other skills do I need to seek out?* Those questions are the first steps to building the team you need to reach your goals.

The first mentors I talked to were very experienced in buying real estate, renovating rental homes, and managing property. These were all areas where I had no experience—and where I had no desire to learn how to do them. Or, more accurately, I had no desire to take all the time it would take to learn how to do these things well. I knew that I couldn't possibly learn the ins and outs of these tasks as quickly as I could find someone with more experience who already had those skills. Instead, I examined the process and took a hard look at what I could contribute to it.

My first potential mentor wasn't interested in working together, but instead I found a husband-and-wife team of a former architect and an accountant who had a lot of experience finding and renovating houses in order to rent them out. I paid them to teach me, and then I figured out the value I brought to the real estate investing process. Combining our strengths created a dream team that's successfully bought, renovated, and rented or sold more than 200 homes in the past 14 years. And our process is something that others can do as well.

THE FOUR FS

The different roles needed to create a successful real estate investment program are based on main steps of the process, which I call the "four Fs." The first is to *find* the property. On its face, this sounds easy. But you're not just finding any property that might be for sale. You need to find a property that you can buy at a discount, and one that is certain to provide cash flow once you've renovated it. Finding the right property involves knowing the real estate market in the area and knowing the right price for both purchase and renovations. What kind of deal can you get? How much can you expect to make in rent? How in-demand is the area?

The second step in the process is to secure *financing*. Once your team has found the right property, you have to find a way to pay not just for the house, but also for the improvements you need to make on it. And because you are only going to buy older properties that need some work so you can get a good deal, some kind of renovation is always going to be necessary.

When you've found and financed the property, you can start the most labor-intensive part of the process: *fixing up* the property. A lot can go wrong at this stage, so in order to avoid nasty—and expensive—surprises, it's essential to get a thorough inspection of any property before you close on it, so you go into it with a clear idea of what work is necessary and what potential problems there might be. Relatively simple and inexpensive cosmetic upgrades like paint and flooring are going to give you a lot more return on your investment than something time- and budget-consuming like taking down walls or reconfiguring layouts. Your only goal is getting the property in good enough shape that someone is willing to pay rent to live there—you're not renovating it to meet your own personal design tastes or desires.

The final step in the process is all about the cash *flow*. That means ensuring you have a property manager in place to find a solid renter and handle all the business of lease agreements, references, deposits, and rent collection. This is where the money starts coming in. But if you're working with a team, it's also when the possibility of disputes becomes more serious. You need to make sure you have all agreed on how the money is divided and how everyone is paid.

Being responsible for all four Fs would be overwhelming for almost anyone, which is most of the reason so few people take on rental properties. It's much more realistic to look at the pieces of the process and figure out where best your personal skills fit. Once you focus on just one part that you can do well and seek out a team to help with the other steps, the load is much lighter and the process feels a lot more manageable.

For me, my banking background and familiarity with securing financing meant that I could bring a substantial amount of knowledge to the finance step of the process. Once I aligned myself with people who were adept at the other three Fs, we hit the ground running.

HOW IT WORKED FOR ME

Everyone has their own experience and your background is likely different from mine, but that doesn't mean my experience isn't useful in helping you map out your own approach.

That's particularly true if the part of the process you'd like to be involved in is that of a passive investor, who reaps the benefits with minimal work.

My break into investing in rental property came from a refusal. I had met a man through my work who did that kind of work, and I admired how successful he had been. But, when I asked him if he would teach me, he said no. I was surprised because we'd always been friendly, and I knew he respected me professionally. But he also knew his own strengths, and teaching was not one of them. He didn't just turn me away, however. He told me about a couple who bought, renovated, and rented homes in the area who had begun a local mentorship program.

The cost for six classes with them was $6,000. That was a large investment, but after doing some research on the couple and their work, I signed up. The way I saw it, the six classes I would get for that investment were going to compress time, so I could learn quickly rather than slowly. They were going to help me avoid making major mistakes that could potentially cost much more than $6,000. And aligning myself with people who knew the industry and the market seemed like a great opportunity to see what doors it could open for me.

Most of their other students I met at the classes were people thinking about acquiring a handful of properties—one to three houses maybe—and then being done. I was already thinking on a bigger scale. Once I identified the value I could bring to the process by being able to arrange financing for myself or for other investors, I approached my mentors and proposed an idea. They would keep doing all the work they'd been doing—finding the properties, renovating the properties, and managing the rentals—but they wouldn't have to put one dime of their own money into the property.

I knew how banking worked, so I knew that taking out a loan to purchase a house that needed work and had no rental agreement in place was not a loan that a banker would want to make. But I could see another method of financing that *would* work: finding people who had the money available—either as cash in their account or a credit line they could open—and using that investment to finance the process up-front. I would bring investors and help arrange financing while my partners dealt with the actual properties. We hammered out a division of profits that would be fair to them, to me, and to our investors, and we got started.

We've stuck to the same process for 14 years. Each time I bring in a new investor, we create a general partnership or a partnership agreement with them that was prepared by a real estate attorney. We use that same agreement over and over to guide us on the properties we purchase with each investor.

My first investor was my neighbor. My sister was the second. Other investors have been friends from college or customers I met through banks I had previously worked at. I don't need to attract a lot of new investors, but if someone brings up the subject of real estate investment, I'm always happy to explain the process. To date, I've partnered with about 15 investors, and none of them have failed to make money. All they have to do is sit back and wait for their checks.

FINDING THE RIGHT PEOPLE

Some of my success in the real estate market comes from my banking experience and contacts, of course, but it's not necessary to have a financial background. It's much more important to put in the work to find the right people to partner with. Even if I didn't have my connections, I'd still be out there doing my due diligence and searching for potential partners. Those are people who are already successfully involved in the process whose skills complement the skills you've figured out you can bring to it.

An excellent resource for starting the process is the real estate investing community at BiggerPockets.com. They host a weekly podcast, and their website is full of useful information and has a forum where you can ask and answer questions. It's the best way to find local groups in your area and people who might be interested in working with real estate investors. I wouldn't recommend jumping in and giving money to the first person you meet—obviously—but this is a way you can start to explore the resources available, learn more about individuals doing similar work in your area, and explore your options with people you know are as invested in the process as you are.

It probably goes without saying, but if you're getting to know someone as a potential business partner, start small. Just try one house together as a test case to see whether you can work together and might be able to form a partnership going forward. Agree before you start on how the house will be titled after you purchase it and how both of you are secure for collateral and cash invested—and have an exit strategy prepared just in case the whole thing turns into a disaster. The more emotion and tension you can eliminate by planning up-front, the less drama will unfold throughout the project. You have to protect yourself and your investment, but you also have to recognize that whoever you are partnering with deserves that same protection.

If you have a plan going in and a just-in-case plan ready if you both need to get out, that will minimize the risk, but keep in mind that this is the best way to make sure that you're working with people who have a similar approach to you in terms of culture and goals. If they're thinking of working on one or two houses over the next five years, and you're thinking of buying 10 houses in the next two years, you probably aren't the right partners.

I recommend keeping the team as small as possible, perhaps around two or three partners max. For one thing, that will make it easier to keep everyone aligned. For another, the more partners there are, the smaller the percentage of profits for everyone. The key is to make sure they're the *right* people doing the *right* parts of the process—then you can all trust each other to do your specific jobs.

That removes most heartache and stress from the project before you even start, but the popular image of the real estate and rental market is still that it's full of potential nightmares. Let's see what are the worst things that can happen and how you can guard against them.

CHAPTER 7

FACE THE FEAR

REAL ESTATE INVESTING IS NOT without its risks. I've had my share of unfortunate experiences, many of which can be outside our control, like nightmare tenants or acts of nature. Once you own more than one or two properties, it's not a question of if you will have an unfortunate experience affect you, but a question of when. The only thing you can do is to make sure you learn from them every time.

My worst experience to date involved a fire. My partners and I had just closed on a four-unit building, the investor was on board, the tenants were lined up and moved in, and from my point of view, the project was solid. All we had to do was collect the rent. Then, 30 days later, the building was destroyed by fire. Nobody was harmed, which was the main thing, and the property was insured with a policy that covered not only the costs of restoring the property, but also the rent we missed while the tenants were displaced.

That was the main thing I took from the experience: the value of having the right policy with a good insurance company. It might sound obvious, but it continues to be one of my number-one tips to new investors. Any insurance company will write policies and cash checks for premium payments, but you only find out if you have a good insurance company when it comes to claim filing and timely payment of coverage—that's where you discover if you're aligned with the right company and the right agent. If you are, then this becomes less of an issue.

With this particular house, there was an issue with how the policy was titled, which was an irritant that took a letter from our attorney to resolve. But the claim was eventually paid in full, which mitigated our losses on the fire. However, in the time it took the payment to come through, the area had been updated on new flood zone maps, and the property was now in a flood zone. This meant that we either needed to raise the building by six feet to get it out of the flood zone, or we needed to demolish it. In fact, my partners and I chose to sell the property "as-is," which was burned out and with no tenants in place. It wasn't what we had intended, but thanks to the insurance payout and to doing our due diligence on the original purchase, we profited by about $30,000 and were happy to move on.

EXPECTATIONS AND OPPORTUNITIES

That situation, with the fire and the flood zone, was irritating, but we were prepared. We had a plan, which was to make sure we were insured, and we found solutions as problems arose. Being nimble is just a part of the process. Stuff happens with houses, and some of it is bad. Can you avoid that completely? It's impossible. But you can plan for it and have realistic expectations.

Fear and apprehension are normal feelings when approaching something new and something as involved as investing in real estate. But just because you are afraid of something doesn't mean you shouldn't do it. I tend to believe the old adage that fear is nothing more than "false evidence appearing real." Feeling the fear is normal—but letting the fear dictate your choices will only have the effect of limiting your opportunities. There are lots of reasons why people don't get into property renovation and management, and some of them are valid...but fear doesn't have to be one of them. You can mitigate virtually all the risks you're likely to meet.

In all my 14 years of real estate investing, the fire is the one major event that really sidetracked our original plans. Other than that, it's been a fairly smooth experience. Even through the fallout of the COVID-19 pandemic, I adjusted my expectations (downward, of course!) and the effects of the lockdowns and the economic downturn turned out to be not nearly as bad as I had anticipated. After all, in the end, everybody still needs a place to live.

If I can get through that, that's evidence to underline the fact that I need to feel the fear, but I don't need to let it control my choices.

My initial fear of investing in real estate was primarily related to one of the most common fears that stops people getting involved: fear of debt. Unless you're already wealthy, you'll have to fund your investment by borrowing money. Throughout my life, I had been conditioned to believe that borrowing money was inherently negative. To my parents' generation, this was their bedrock principle.

Things have changed a lot since then. I recently had to complete a financial statement, and my banker friend I was dealing with thought I'd made an error when he saw that I had listed my contingent liabilities as $8 million. "That can't be right," he said. But it was. My partners and I have personally guaranteed real estate loans totaling over $8 million.

"How do you sleep at night?" he asked, aghast that anyone owed such an amount. "Just fine," I replied. "Because those loans are secured by $16 million in real estate." Even if the market crashed by 50 percent—which is so unlikely you can discount it as a possibility—I could still sell everything and still be fine. After all, with regards to how much debt you can repay in a worst-case scenario, you can drown in three feet of water just as easily as you can drown in the ocean.

For me, owning more properties helps me deal with the fear, because it gives me the chance to mitigate the risk by spreading it out over numerous properties to lessen the impact. If you own just a handful of houses (up to five, say), and one of them is damaged by a fire or a flood, that's 20 percent of your assets impacted. If you own dozens of properties and one is damaged, that's a far smaller portion of your assets. It's still a problem in need of a solution, but the burden is easier to bear because you're only losing a small share of your rental income and the value of your other properties will offset it.

PROBLEMS HAVE SOLUTIONS

Any time there's a problem, there is a potential solution. Of course you should always hope for smooth sailing, but hope alone isn't going to see you through. You also need to plan ahead and align yourself with the right team. You need the right insurance company, the right real estate agent, the right contractor, the right property manager. If you have the right people in place, you've done all you can to protect yourself and your investment. Now you just need to rely on common sense and ensure that you have realistic expectations.

Going into your first property, be honest with yourself about what to expect. If it breaks even, you'll have done well. You certainly won't realize your full wealth potential on that first property—not even close—but that's the price of entry. You'll learn a vast amount of information about the process, about the people you've aligned yourself with, and about yourself. If you break even or come out owing something, just think of it as the cost of your education. The only way someone would be disappointed with a result like that—and I mean seriously disappointed—would be if they had incredibly unrealistic expectations going in. Go in with the right team, a little bit of positive thinking balanced by a healthy amount of fear and realism, and the knowledge that problems that arise will simply be resolved in the process of learning how things work in the real world.

Real estate is not magic, but it's not rocket science either. The benefit of investing in real estate rather than having all your eggs in traditional retirement funds or the stock market is that, even when things go sideways, you have a tangible piece of property that still has value. Even if that property gets damaged—by fire or flood, or even by unruly tenants—it's still there and it's still yours. Dealing with any problems might be a headache, but wouldn't you rather have an asset that can be sold than have nothing to show for your efforts? In a worst-case scenario, that's what happens when a stock investment tanks: you get left with a piece of paper showing what you once had but don't have any more. You might avoid insurance claims or dealing with repairs, true, but you'll have to start over from scratch.

Owning a house that's already built and renting it out is the simplest, easiest business to understand. It's also an asset that will always be in demand. Everyone needs to live somewhere. Just about everybody's paying rent or a mortgage to someone. If you live in a rental and pay rent on a lease, whoever owns that property is making money. If you're buying a house and have a mortgage, the mortgage company is making money. Housing is virtually always a source of financial benefit for someone. Why not make that someone you?

If the potential problems put you off, think about your regular job. You likely deal with problems all the time, both big and small. If something goes wrong, you don't throw your hands in the air and quit. You solve the problem. That's part of how we earn money: we make plans, do research, and whenever a problem arises, we find a solution.

PLAN AHEAD

Almost always, the best way to avoid problems is to avoid cutting corners. One thing I've learned in my years of experience is that the shorter or easier route is likely not the one that will get you where you want to go unscathed. You always end up paying for doing things the wrong way, such as not ensuring you are aligned with your team and your goals.

Renovating older homes for rent has been done millions of times by millions of people, so almost all the mistakes that can be made have likely already been made. That means there are people out there who know how to do it correctly—or how to avoid problems in the first place. This is when it's useful to look to those who have experience to guide you. I originally approached my mentors to teach me to do this whole process myself, but when I saw how they made use of professionals they could trust—people they'd worked with and vetted over years of trial and error—I decided it was better for me to figure out a way I could use their experience to steer clear of disaster.

Fear comes from the unknown. None of us can know everything, so there is always something to fear. But there's always more knowledge to learn, and that knowledge will reduce the fear. One surefire way to achieve that is to align yourself with people who know what you don't or can't know. Another way is to go into the process with your eyes wide open and follow a few basic rules:

- Do your due diligence.
- Don't buy the first house you see.
- Keep things simple.
- Target an area within 5 or 10 miles of where you live or work.
- Find a neighborhood or part of town that's appreciating and compare properties against each other until you find a winner.

- Don't close on anything until all your inspections are done.
- Use screening agencies to avoid taking in a bad tenant.
- Check potential tenants' previous rental payment history, income, criminal records, etc.

Information gathering is just one way to reduce potential pitfalls. Another is to make sure you have good systems in place to make sure that, while the things that go wrong teach you to be a better investor, you also learn how not to make the same mistakes again. That way, unexpected problems don't destroy your investment program—and the potential benefits far outweigh the possible downsides.

CHAPTER 8
THE NEXT STEP

AT THE START OF THIS BOOK, I asked you to plug in your numbers to the Money Scoreboard and decide if you were happy with where you are, based on what you've saved so far for your retirement. It's something that I'd encourage everyone to ask themselves, because the answer will likely bring them up short.

When I looked at my own money scoreboard in my 40s, I was shocked at how far behind I was. I'd worked my whole life, I'd contributed to a retirement fund and to social security, but when I did the math, I was nowhere near where I needed to be. I had done everything I'd seen previous generations do. I'd followed the path laid before me—before everyone—and it simply wasn't taking me where I wanted to go. My retirement savings simply did not match up to the lifestyle I wanted to maintain in retirement. That's when I set out to find an alternative, something that would set me up to live well now while I could build wealth to prepare myself for retirement—and that's exactly what I found when I fully committed to real estate investing.

The majority of middle-aged, middle-class Americans are in the same boat I was—and many don't even realize it. But through real estate investments and owning rental properties, those same middle-aged, middle-class Americans can leverage their skills and their credit to change their financial future, creating passive income that can benefit them both now and in retirement. They can jump from being stuck in the middle class to becoming a millionaire just like I did.

Because of the investments I've made and the system I've established for myself and my partners, I could retire right now if I wanted to—but I'll let you in on a secret: I will never retire! I enjoy working in the bank, and I also enjoy the work of real estate investing. The two fit well with my life right now, and the financial benefits they bring will last for many years.

In this book, I wanted to show you how real estate investing can be a reliable way—perhaps the most reliable way—to use your money passively to generate income now and to continue to fund your retirement. Take it from me, it works. And take it from me, too, that you really need to do it. I see enough middle-class Americans' financial statements to know that, as a generation, we're a long way off where we need to be. There's a massive shortfall between what people have and what they will need for income. This retirement income crisis is coming down the track, and it is going to run people over like a freight train.

THE PRESENT AND THE FUTURE

The Money Scoreboard tells us where we are now, and that's the first step to figuring out where we'll be in the future. Do you have the wealth you'll need to maintain your lifestyle? Do you have a passive income stream established that will help you save now and pay your expenses when you no longer work full-time? I didn't. But I do now.

For many of us, traditional retirement planning was the only option we knew to prepare for the years after we stop working, but it's not a reliable way to build wealth. Traditional investing is inherently insecure—so why would you trust it with 100 percent of your financial assets to set you up for the financial security you need?

The only secure way I've found to build wealth and passive income for your retirement years—and I've looked hard at all sorts of alternative investments—is real estate investing in rental properties. It's one of the few investment categories that promises both a revenue stream and capital appreciation that can match your needs in retirement.

Many people can see the obvious attractions with real estate, but they're hesitant to become involved. The main reason they're resistant is usually because they are afraid of debt. We've been culturally conditioned to believe that owing money is inherently bad. That traditional attitude toward debt is not an excuse not to become involved. That mindset needs to be shifted to embrace the borrowing power at our fingertips. The beauty of leveraging your credit to buy real estate is that you're using other people's money: the debt doesn't get paid by you, personally; rather, the tenant pays the loan back with their rent.

People are also afraid of the potential downfalls of managing rental properties, from natural disasters to nightmare renters. Maybe that comes from TV reality shows or from apocryphal stories, but the reality is that most of the worst-case scenarios you're afraid of are unlikely ever to happen. If you set up a process and align yourself with the right team, you can face the fear and do it anyway—because you and your team know that you're ready to address any problems that come your way.

The key to success in this kind of investing is to play to your strengths and find the right people to work with. You can concentrate on the parts of the process you enjoy or choose to play a more passive role, if that's what you're interested in. It's your choice. Figure out where you add value to the process and build a team around you to complete the other steps in the process. There are other people out there doing this already; find them and join them, which is how I started.

No investment of any kind is without any risk—otherwise everyone would be doing it because it would be the fabled "money for nothing." But with real estate investing, unlike stock market and traditional savings accounts, you have a tangible piece of property to show for your investment. Having something physical to show for your efforts, something that will appreciate in value no matter what, is the best way to set yourself up for the future you want. You're receiving rental payments *and* you're accruing appreciation in the value of the property. It's an investment win–win.

Real estate investment is like the *Moneyball* concept in baseball. It's not about hitting home runs or recruiting the flashiest players; it's about setting yourself up for wins by building a team that's going to consistently get on first base. You may never hit a home run, but getting base hit after base hit is going to accumulate, which is going to build your score on the Money Scoreboard. In time, that accumulates value and eventually makes you a winner.

THE NEXT STEP

Appreciate the scale of the problem you face, but be optimistic. If you can overcome the self-limitations that might make you reluctant to become involved in real estate, the system I've shared in this book can indeed make you a middle-class millionaire—at almost any stage of your life.

You just need to get started.

I've given you the structure of my program and tips on what you need to do. There are more resources at the back of the book and on my website, www.MoneyScoreboard.com. So make a commitment to start exploring, learning about the business of investing in real estate, and reaching out to potential partners. Unleash your true economic potential—and make yourself a millionaire!

APPENDIX
MONEY SCOREBOARD DATA SHEET

HOW DO YOU KNOW where you are on the Money Scoreboard? The best way is to fill in a table like the one I use to evaluate my customers in the bank. Add the data and follow the instructions to figure out your financial position.

MIDDLE CLASS TO MILLIONAIRE

Money Scoreboard Asset Inventory List

Annual Passive Income	Amount	Notes
Interest Earned – 2020	1,545	
Dividends Paid – 2020	–	
Capital Gains from sales	–	
Net Real Estate Income	–	
Other Passive Income	–	Source = N/A
Total Passive Income	1,545	

Asset Inventory	Amount	Notes
Annual Income	247,260	
Credit Score	778	
Home Equity	20,000	See "Home Equity Calculation" below
Asset Inventory Calculation:		
Home Equity Line of Credit	20,000	Balance Available to Draw Out at 0.00%
Retirement Account	91,470	
Emergency Fund	–	
Health Savings Account	8,572	Interest Rate on Health Savings Account = 0.1%
Cash for Investing – Savings	50,000	Interest Rate on Savings = 0.5%
Other Savings	–	
Cash Surrender Value – Life Insurance	–	
Unsecured Line of Credit	30,000	Rate = 10.00%
Credit Cards	7,700	(Available credit/balance transfer at teaser rate)
Potential Cash for Investing in Real Estate	207,742	

Other Capital Sources	Amount	Notes
Personal Loans from Friends/Family	–	
Loan from 401(k)	–	
Brokerage Account – Margin Loan	–	
Total	–	

Home Equity Calculation	Amount	Notes
Current Value	400,000	
80% Loan To Value	320,000	
Less: Mortgage Balance	(300,000)	
Equity Available	20,000	

MONEY SCOREBOARD DATA SHEET

Passive Income Calculation

Grade on Retirement Savings	
Current Age	33
Money Scoreboard Quarter	Q1
Total Retirement Savings	91,470
Average Annual Amount Saved	11,434
Annual Gross Income	**247,260**

Years Until Expenses Covered by P.I.
423

Annual Savings:	
Retirement/401(k)	12,000
Emergency Fund	–
Health Savings Acct	6,000
Other Savings – Monthly Surplus	36,000
Total Savings	**54,000**

Income – Savings = Annual Expenses	193,260

Assets Needed To Cover Expenses	4,831,500
Cash Flow Average Annual Return	4%

ANNUAL PASSIVE INCOME
$1,545

ANNUAL EXPENSES
$193,260

PASSIVE INCOME SURPLUS/SHORTAGE
–$191,715

ANNUAL PASSIVE INCOME

1. **Interest earned:** Record the amount of interest earned with the money kept in bank savings accounts, certificates of deposit, money market accounts, and any interest earned from money you lent out to family or friends.

2. **Dividends paid:** Record any dividends received from stocks you own in a brokerage account or paid to you from a life insurance company on permanent insurance.

3. **Capital gains from sales:** Record any profit made on selling stocks or real estate. If several stocks were sold, and some lost money, deduct the losses from the profits and record the net result.

4. **Net real estate income:** Record net cash flow to you after all debt is paid, including property taxes, insurance, repairs and maintenance.

5. **Other passive income:** Record the source and amount of any income you received that is not job-related and does not require any of your time for you to get paid.

6. **Total passive income:** Add up all of the above for your total.

ASSET INVENTORY

1. **Annual gross income:** Record your gross income before taxes.

2. **Credit score:** Record your FICO score or go to www.freecreditreport.com and pull your one free credit report to find your credit score.

3. **Home equity:** Refer to the Home Equity Calculation section for instructions on calculating this.

4. **Home equity line of credit:** Record the total home equity line of credit balance available to borrow here.

5. **Retirement account(s):** Record the total amount in all retirement accounts from the last statement for your IRA, Roth IRA, 401(k), 403(b), SEP-IRA, etc.

6. **Emergency fund:** Record the balance in your emergency fund if kept separate from your checking and savings accounts.

7. **Health savings account:** Record the balance from your last statement.

8. **Cash for investing (savings):** Record the balance in this account if separate from your checking account.

9. **Other savings:** Record the balance and source for any non-bank savings accounts.
10. **Cash surrender value (life insurance):** Record the cash surrender value of any permanent insurance you own.
11. **Unsecured line of credit:** Record the available balance that could be borrowed today and the interest rate the lender is charging you.
12. **Credit cards:** Record the available balance that has a low teaser rate offer for all credit cards combined.

Potential cash for investing: Add up all of the above for your total.

OTHER CAPITAL SOURCES

1. **Personal loans from friends/family:** If you needed to borrow money at an interest rate comparable to a bank loan (4.25 percent or less), how much money would a friend or family member lend you? Record the total from all sources.
2. **Loan from 401(k):** If your current employer allows loans from your retirement plan, call your HR department to find out if you are eligible and how much you could borrow. Record the total in this box.

Brokerage account (margin loan): If you have an account with a brokerage company (TD Ameritrade, Charles Schwab, E-Trade, etc.) and have stocks, how much would they allow you to borrow against those stocks? Record the total in this box.

HOME EQUITY CALCULATION

1. **Current value:** If you sold your home today, what would it sell for? If you don't know, record what you paid for the house.

80 percent loan to value: Multiply the amount for your home's current value by 80 percent to get this calculation.

Example: Your house is worth $225,000 × .80 = $180,000 loan to value.

2. **Less—mortgage balance:** Record the balance owed on the house from your last mortgage statement.

Equity available: Subtract the loan to value figure (line 2 above) from the current value of the house (line 1 above) to get the equity available. Record this figure here and also on line 3 of the Asset Inventory section.

Example: Your loan to value is $180,000 and your mortgage balance is $155,000, so your equity available is $25,000. ($180,000 − $155,000 = $25,000).

GRADE ON RETIREMENT SAVINGS

1. **Current age:** Record your current age.
2. **Money Scoreboard quarter:** Record which quarter you are in based on your age:

MONEY SCOREBOARD DATA SHEET

    a. Q1 = 25 to 34

    b. Q2 = 35 to 44

    c. Q3 = 45 to 54

    d. Q4 = 55 to 65

3. **Total retirement savings:** Line 5 of Asset Inventory
4. **Average annual amount saved:** Take annual gross income from Asset Inventory (line 1) and subtract total savings (line 5 from the next section). Divide that figure by the difference between your current age and 25.

Example: If your annual gross income is $60,000 and you are saving roughly 10 percent per year ($60,000 × .10 = $6,000) then you would be spending the remainder, which is $54,000 ($60,000 − $6,000 = $54,000).

ANNUAL SAVINGS SECTION

1. **Retirement/401(k):** Record how much you contribute to your retirement per year and include the employer's match if you are 100 percent vested.
2. **Emergency fund:** Record how much you contribute per year to this account.
3. **Health savings account:** Record how much you contribute per year to this account.
4. **Other savings (monthly surplus):** Record any other savings that are not spent on bills each month.
5. **Total savings:** Record the total of lines 1 through 4 above.

CALCULATE YOUR SCORE

1. **Income – savings = annual expenses:** Take the total savings from line 5 above and subtract from the annual gross income (line 1 of Asset Inventory) to get annual expenses and record here.

2. **Assets needed to cover expenses:** Take the annual expenses from above and multiply it by .04 to get the total assets needed to cover expenses.

Example: Total annual expenses are $54,000 ÷ .04 = $1,350,000

1. **Years until expenses covered by passive income:** Take assets needed to cover expenses and divide by average annual amount saved from line 4 of Grade on Retirement Savings, which gives the number of years it will take (if no changes are made) to save the amount needed to cover your monthly expenses.

Example: Total assets needed to cover expenses is $1,350,000 ÷ $6,000 = 189 years!

1. **Passive income surplus/shortage:** Take the total passive income from line 6 of the Annual Passive Income section, and subtract the annual expenses from line 1 of this section to get the surplus or shortage of passive income.

Example: Say annual passive income is $1,500 – $54,000 = -$52,500, which is a shortage.

RESOURCES

THESE ARE SOME HELPFUL RESOURCES for further education, mentoring, and webinars to teach you more about how to get started with investing in real estate to generate passive income to replace or enhance your earned income:

BOOKS

- *Rich Dad Poor Dad* by Robert Kiyosaki and Sharon L. Lechter
- *Rich Dad's Cashflow Quadrant: Guide to Financial Freedom* by Robert Kiyosaki
- *The Millionaire Real Estate Investor* by Gary Keller
- *The Book on Rental Property Investing: How to Create Wealth and Passive Income Through Smart Buy & Hold Real Estate Investing* by Brandon Turner
- *Tribe of Millionaires: What If One Choice Could Change Everything?* by David Osborn, Pat Hiban, Mike McCarthy, and Tim Rhode

PODCASTS

- *Bigger Pockets*: www.biggerpockets.com, David Greene and Rob Abasolo
- *The Real Estate Guys Radio Show*: www.realestateguysradio.com, Robert Helms and Russell Gray
- *The Real Wealth Show*: www.realwealth.com, Kathy Fettke
- *Tribe of Millionaires*: www.tribeofmillionaires.com, Jamie Gruber

MEETINGS AND MASTERMINDS

- Gobundance Emerge program: www.gobundanceemerge.com
- Real Estate Investment Network (REIN): Search Google to find the nearest local group.

MENTORSHIP OR REAL ESTATE PARTNERSHIP

- www.MoneyScoreboard.com: Get in touch with the author of *Middle Class to Millionaire*, David Vernich.